GREG
MADDUX

(Photo on front cover.)

Maddux pitches a shut out against the Chicago Cubs.

(Photo on previous pages.)

Maddux throws against the New York Mets.

Photography supplied by Wide World Photos Inc.

Library of Congress Cataloging-in-Publication Data
Rambeck, Richard.
Greg Maddux / Richard Rambeck
p. cm.
Summary: A biography of the Atlanta Braves' pitcher who was
named baseball's Player of the Year in 1995.
ISBN 1-56766-314-1 (hard cover; lib. bdg..)

1. Maddux, Greg, 1966 -   --Juvenile literature. 2. Baseball
players --United States --Biography --Juvenile literature.
3. Pitchers (Baseball)--United States --Biography --Juvenile
literature. 4. Atlanta Braves (Baseball team)--Juvenile literature.
[1. Maddux, Greg, 1966. – . 2. Baseball players.]
I. Title
GV865.M319R35   1996   96-14644
796.357'092— dc20   CIP
[B]   AC

GREG
MADDUX

BY RICHARD RAMBECK

When they went to the World Series in 1995, the Cleveland Indians brought one of the best-hitting clubs in the history of baseball. As a team, the Indians batted .291, easily the top average in the majors for the year. One Cleveland player, left fielder Albert Belle, had 50 homers and 52 doubles during the regular season. Four other Indians hit at least 20 home runs each. In game one of the World Series, Cleveland faced the Atlanta Braves and their outstanding pitcher, Greg Maddux. The Indians never had a chance.

It was as if Maddux turned Cleveland's powerful bats into sawdust. In nine innings, the Indians got only two hits off Maddux. Cleveland batters hit only four balls out of the infield during the entire game. Maddux, who rarely walks a batter, didn't have any bases on balls. If it hadn't been for two Atlanta errors, the Indians probably wouldn't even have scored. As it was, Atlanta won 3-2, giving Maddux his first-ever World Series victory. The Braves went on to win the series in six games.

After the season, baseball writers voted unanimously to give Maddux the National League's Cy Young Award, which goes to the top pitcher in each league. It was the fourth year in a row that Maddux had received the award. No pitcher in either league had ever won more than two Cy Youngs in a row. Maddux won three Cy Youngs while pitch-

ing for Atlanta and another when he was with the Chicago Cubs. After the 1992 season, Maddux signed with the Braves as a free agent.

"I'm probably more excited about what the team did (in 1995) than winning the Cy Young," Maddux said of the World Series-winning Braves. "I think it's harder to win a world title than the Cy Young. But this one (the 1995 Cy Young) has to be the most special because of the world title." In late 1995, Greg Maddux became the first pitcher ever to be named baseball's Player of the Year by the Associated Press. There was little doubt he was the best pitcher in baseball and maybe one of the best in history.

It's hard to believe how great a year Maddux had in 1995. He led the National League in wins (19), earned run average (1.63), and complete games (10). He was tied for the lead in shutouts (3) and innings pitched (209 2/3). Maddux also was third in the league in strikeouts (181) and he isn't really a strikeout pitcher. In addition, for the sixth time, he won the Gold Glove Award as the top fielding pitcher in the National League.

Four-time Cy Young winner Greg Maddux pitches against the Los Angeles Dodgers.

Maddux was almost unbeatable in 1995, posting a 19-2 record. In fact, he's been almost unbeatable since the 1992 season. During his four Cy Young seasons, he had a total record of 75-29

and an ERA of 1.98. He had the lowest ERA in the National League in 1993, 1994, and 1995. In addition, in 1995 he became the first major leaguer since Walter Johnson in 1919 to have two straight seasons with ERAs of less than 1.80.

What makes Greg Maddux so good? What's the secret behind his four straight Cy Youngs? Quite simply, he can throw the ball where he wants, when he wants, practically all the time. During the 1995 season, he walked only 23 batters in 209 2/3 innings. That's fewer than one batter a game. Most great pitchers are happy if they walk only two or three batters every nine innings. Also in 1995, Maddux went 51 innings without walking anyone. The streak started June 3 and ended July 13. That's 40 days between walks!

Greg Maddux needs to have control over his pitches because he doesn't throw the ball all that hard. He's not a big, strong rocket-thrower like Roger Clemens or Randy Johnson. Instead, he's an average-sized man. Maddux is six feet tall, and 175 pounds. He wears glasses when he's not pitching. Maddux, in fact, looks more like a high school English teacher than the best pitcher in baseball. Former Atlanta pitcher Don Sutton said Maddux "goes to class for four days [when he's not pitching], then teaches the class on the fifth day."

Former Atlanta catcher Charlie O'Brien said he rarely had to move his mitt when Maddux was pitching because Maddux would hit the target almost every time. "He's a master," St. Louis manager Mike Jorgenson said after Maddux threw a two-hit, no-walk shutout against the Cardinals in 1995. "He puts every pitch almost exactly where he wants to. That's one tough guy to go up against." Maddux, however, wasn't always so tough. He struggled early in his career.

In 1987 Maddux had a 6-14 record with the Chicago Cubs. He wasn't a great pitcher; he wasn't even a good pitcher. Maddux said that, among other problems that year, he forgot how to throw his change-up. "I think when you come up and you're young, you think you're on top of the world," he said. "I think you do a lot of stupid things, and I did my share of those my first couple of years (in the majors). Hopefully, I've learned from them." Apparently, he has.

Maddux doesn't forget how to throw his change-up anymore. Nor does he forget how to throw any of his other four pitches—a slider, a curve, and two kinds of fastball. Now Maddux is like a machine, throwing each pitch the same way every time. "You could take 1,000 pictures of his delivery, and they'd all be the

same," says San Francisco Giants pitching coach Dick Pole, who was a coach with the Chicago Cubs when Maddux pitched for that team.

"**H**e always throws his pitch, instead of what the batter wants to hit," Charlie O'Brien says. "Even if he's behind in the count, he's going to throw his pitch." Maddux, who is called "Mad Dog" by his Atlanta teammates, is never that impressed with himself, despite his many achievements. "No matter what's done in the past," says Atlanta pitching coach Leo Mazzone, "he always thinks he can get better." After Maddux's remarkable 1995 season, that doesn't seem possible.

CHARLEVOIX ELEMENTARY SCHOOL
LIBRARY